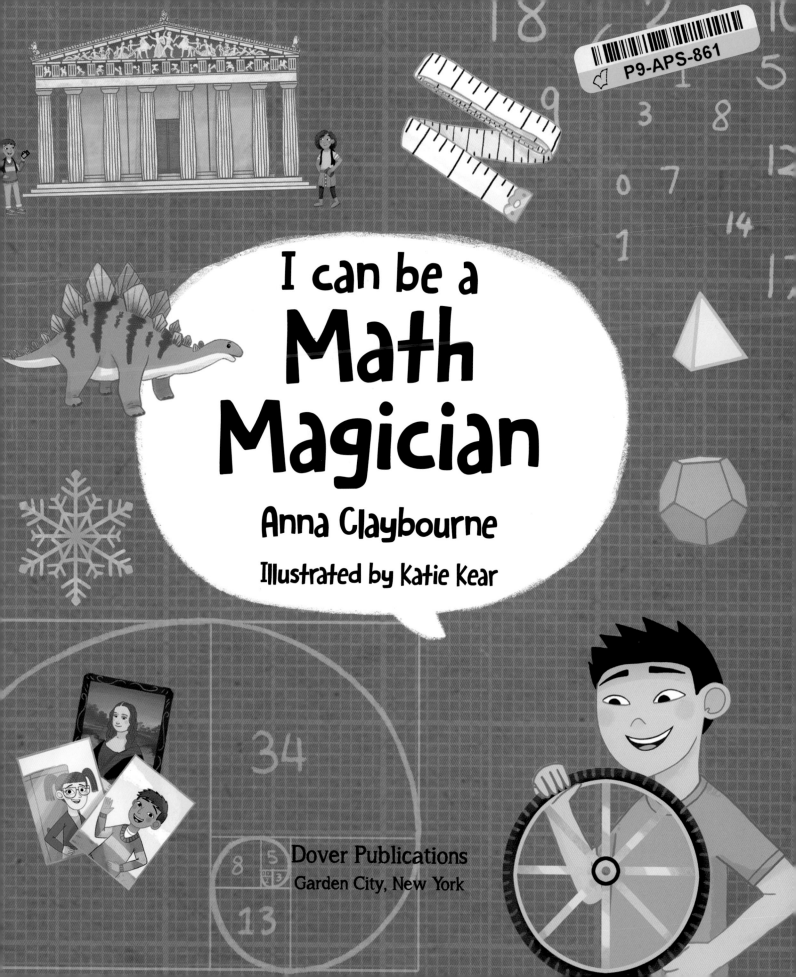

I can be a
Math Magician

Anna Claybourne

Illustrated by Katie Kear

Dover Publications
Garden City, New York

Bibliographical Note

This Dover edition, first published in 2019, is an unabridged republication of the work published by Arcturus Publishing Limited, London, in 2019.

International Standard Book Number

ISBN-13: 978-0-486-83922-6
ISBN-10: 0-486-83922-2

Printed in China by Chang Jiang Printing Media Co., Ltd.
83922206   2023
www.doverpublications.com

What is STEM?

STEM is a world-wide initiative that aims to cultivate an interest in Science, Technology, Engineering, and Mathematics, in an effort to promote these disciplines to as wide a variety of students as possible.

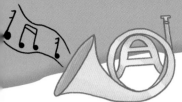

Contents

Numbers Are Everywhere!

Numbers aren't just something you study at school. They're a LOT more than that! In fact, numbers are essential. We use them and rely on them all the time.

Imagine how all these things would work if we didn't have numbers!

Come to my birthday party! June 7 at 3pm

They've won the game 8–5!

I live at number 49, apartment 4.

Now stir in 2 tablespoons of flour ...

And here's your change.

Launching in t minus 15 seconds ...

From buildings, banking, and bus routes to simply knowing what time it is, numbers are everywhere.

Project: Become a Mind Reader

Start with this super-simple number trick. Memorize the steps, then try it on a friend.

First, write the number 5 on a piece of paper (without letting your friend see it). Fold it up, and put it in an envelope.

1. Ask your friend to think of a number .... any number!

2. Ask her to double it ... then add 10 ...

3. Then divide by 2 ... then take away the number she first thought of.

4. Tell her that with your magic powers, you can read her mind and know what number she's ended up with. Hand her the envelope to open.

As the famous mathematician Shakuntala Devi said:

Without mathematics, you can't do anything! Everything around you is mathematics. Everything around you is numbers.

She'll be amazed that you got it right! But the secret to this trick is that whatever number you start with, you'll always end up with five.

Magic Squares

A "magic square" is a square with a pattern of numbers arranged in a grid. If you add up any row of numbers in the grid, you'll always get the same answer. Magic squares have been around for thousands of years and feature in the ancient Chinese legend of Lo Shu …

This became known as a "Lo Shu square," or magic square. The number that the rows, columns, and diagonals all add up to (15 in this case) is called the "Magic equation."

Long ago, the rivers in China flooded. After people left offerings by the River Lo, a turtle crept from the water with a strange pattern of dots on its back. The dots stood for nine different numbers, arranged in a square. Every single row of numbers in the square added up to 15. The people took it as a message from the river telling them to leave 15 offerings.

			=15
4	9	2	=15
3	5	7	=15
8	1	6	=15
=15	=15	=15	=15

Activity: Squares to Solve

The pattern on the turtle's back isn't the only kind of magic square. There are many more, with different patterns, numbers, and sizes. A 3 x 3 square is called an "Order 3" magic square. A 4 x 4 square is called an "Order 4" magic square, and so on.

A: Magic equation = 12

3	2	7
8	4	2
1	6	3

B: Magic equation = 18

5	5	2
5	6	10
8	7	6

C: Magic equation = 34

3	14	4	2
20	9	20	2
10	7	6	10
1	4	4	20

Can you fill in the missing spaces to complete the magic squares? Remember, all the numbers in each square have to be different. The answers are on page 60.

Möbius Mystery

Can you see anything weird about this loop-shaped object? It looks like a simple loop of paper, but it's actually a mysteriously magical mathematical mindbender called a Möbius strip.

One edge

One side

There's only one side! Look at the strip carefully— it's a simple strip, joined into a loop, but with a single twist in it. Imagine running your finger along it. Unlike a normal loop, which has an inside and an outside, a Möbius strip has just one single, continuous surface. You would touch the whole surface of the strip before getting back to where you started.

A Möbius strip has just one edge, running all the way around it.

Mathematical artist M. C. Escher was inspired by this idea. He drew a picture of a Möbius strip with ants crawling around it, like this.

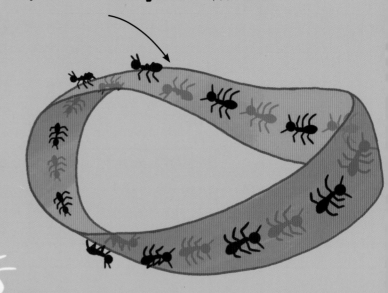

Activity: Make Your Own Möbius Strip

You will need:

- Paper
- Scissors
- Paper glue
- A pen

Make a real-life, 3-dimensional Möbius strip and explore the weirdness for yourself. You can also do an amazing trick with it that will blow your friends' minds!

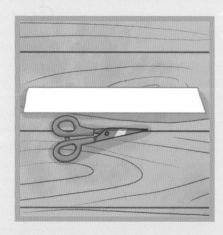

1. Cut a strip of paper about 12 inches (30 cm) long and 1 inch wide (2–3cm).

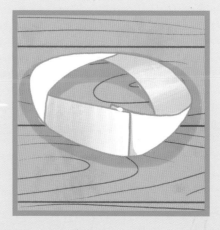

2. Curve the strip into a loop, and line up the ends. Flip one end over. Glue the flat end to the flipped-over end, and hold it until the glue dries.

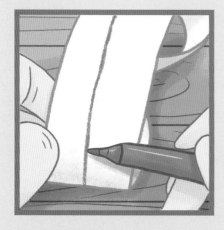

3. Take the pen and draw a line along the middle of the strip. Keep going until you get back to where you started. This shows how the strip has only one side.

4. With your scissors, cut into the middle of the strip, where the line is. Cut all the way along the line to cut the strip in half. What happens?

Magic Multiples

Learning your times tables in school is something every kid has to do. It's true that they can be really useful (in fact, one of the most useful things you'll ever learn!), but remembering all those multiplication tables can be very tricky.

To make it easier, you just need a few mental arithmetic magic tricks!

For the **four** times table, double the number, then double it again.

For example: 6 x 4

Double it: 6 x 2 = 12
Double it again: 12 x 2 = 24

6 x 4 = 24

For the **five** times table, halve the number, then multiply by 10.

For example: 6 x 5

Halve it: Half of 6 = 3
Multiply by 10:   3 x 10 = 30

6 x 5 = 30

For the **nine** times table, you just need 10 fingers.

Put your hands flat in front of you. In your head, number the fingers 1 to 10. To multiply any number by 9, find that finger and fold it down.

Count the number of fingers to the left of it, then the number of fingers to the right of it.

For example: 6 x 9
Fold down finger number 6

6 x 9 = 54

Activity: Two-Hand Calculator

In fact, you can use 10 fingers to multiply together any two numbers from 6 to 10. Once you've learned how it works, try it on the questions below . . .

Hold your hands out with the palms facing you and the fingers pointing toward each other.

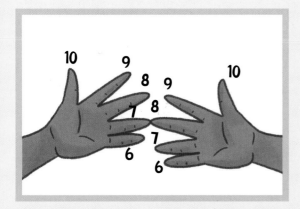

1. Imagine that your fingers are numbered 10, 9, 8, 7, and 6, counting down from the thumbs. To multiply two numbers, touch the corresponding fingers together. For example, 7 x 8.

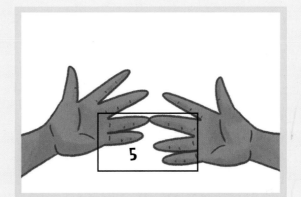

2. Count the two touching fingers and all the fingers below them, and add a zero on the end. In this example, there are 5. Add a zero on the end, which gives us 50.

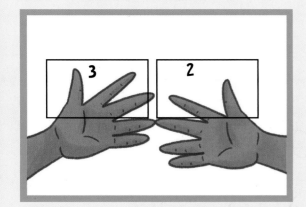

3. Now count the fingers above the touching fingers on both sides, and multiply them together. Here, we get 3 x 2 = 6. Add this to your first number: 50 + 6. And there's the answer! 7 x 8 = 56.

Now use this trick to try these tricky multiples:

6 x 7	9 x 8
8 x 10	10 x 6
7 x 9	7 x 10
9 x 10	9 x 9
6 x 8	6 x 9

Answers are on page 60.

The Golden Ratio

A ratio is a set of numbers that show how different amounts compare. If you have nine apples and six bananas, for example, that's a ratio of 3:2—three apples for every two bananas. One particular ratio is called the "golden ratio."

The second number in this ratio actually goes on forever. But we round it off to about 1:618 to make it easier.

The golden ratio is:

1:1.61803398874989484820 ....

So where does the golden ratio come from? It describes the shape of a particular type of rectangle called the golden rectangle. Its length is 1.618 times its width.

Artists and architects often use the golden rectangle or ratio in their work.

If you cut a square off a golden rectangle, you get another, smaller golden rectangle.

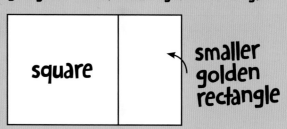

square

smaller golden rectangle

If you cut a square off that smaller rectangle, the same thing happens again— and again and again, on and on forever ...

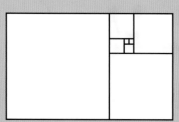

Activity: Draw a Golden Spiral

You can also use the golden ratio to help you draw beautiful spirals.

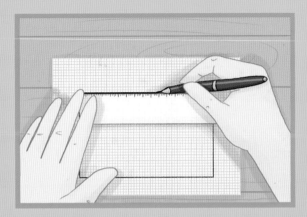

1. First, use a ruler and a pencil to draw a large golden rectangle on a piece of paper.

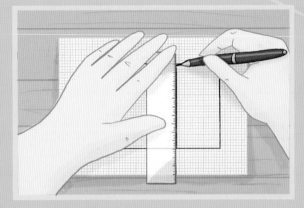

2. Draw the short side first. With a calculator, multiply the length of the short side by 1.618. Use the answer for the length of the long side. Measure and draw a line making a square.

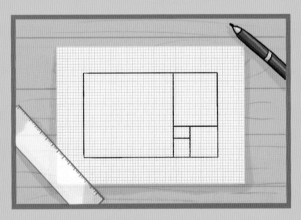

3. Do the same in the smaller golden rectangle And the next one, and the next one, until the rectangles are too small to draw.

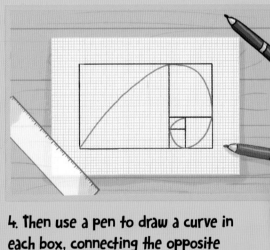

4. Then use a pen to draw a curve in each box, connecting the opposite corners, like this.

Finally, erase the pencil lines for a perfect spiral.

Secret Codes

Since ancient times, we've used numbers to encode things to keep them secret, and we still do today. When people shop online, their payment details are turned into number codes, so that they can be sent over the internet without being stolen.

One simple type of number code uses numbers to stand for letters. For example, you could match letters and numbers in a sequence, like this:

A	B	C	D	E	F	G	H	I	J	K	L	M	N	O	P	Q	R	S	T	U	V	W	X	Y	Z
1	2	3	4	5	6	7	8	9	10	11	12	13	14	15	16	17	18	19	20	21	22	23	24	25	26

Can you decode it?

Then you could write a message using the code, like this:

20 8 1 20   23 1 19   5 1 19 25

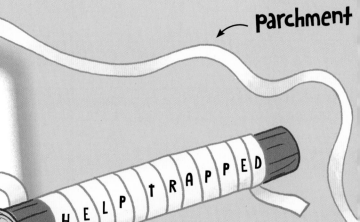

← parchment

The ancient Greeks could make coded messages using a special stick called a scytale. The sender would wrap a strip of parchment around the stick, then write the message along it. A messenger delivered the parchment on its own. Only someone with another scytale the exact same diameter as the first one could wind the strip around it and read the message.

Activity: Cipher Wheel

A cipher wheel lets you use different number codes for different messages—making them extra hard to crack. The sender and receiver of the code each need their own wheel.

You will need:

- Cardstock
- A ruler
- Scissors
- A compass, or round objects to draw around
- A pencil
- A split pin, or prong fastener

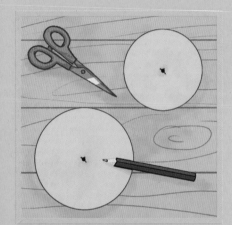

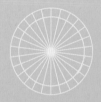

1. Draw two circles on the cardstock, one 4 inches (10cm) across and one 3 inches (8cm) across. Cut them out, and make a hole through the middle of both with the pencil.

2. Draw straight lines across both circles, dividing them into 26 equal sections. (You could trace the picture below to make this easier.)

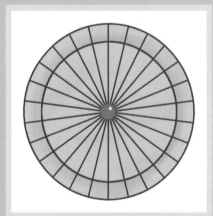

3. Write the 26 letters of the alphabet around the edge of the larger circle and the numbers 1–26 on the smaller circle. Pin the circles together with the fastener.

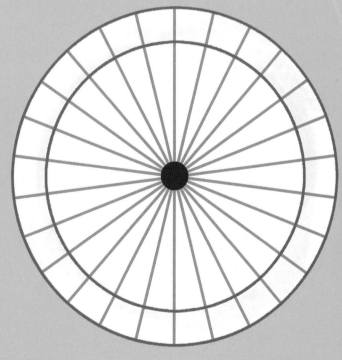

4. Before you write your coded message, make a note of the number that lines up with the letter "A." This is your cipher code! Then write your message, replacing each letter with the corresponding number.

Symmetrical Sides

Symmetry is a feature of shapes. If a shape is symmetrical, it means that one side is a mirror image of the other side. The line down the middle is called the line of symmetry.

Lots of things in real life are symmetrical or almost symmetrical. All regular shapes have at least one line of symmetry.

This shape is not symmetrical! You can't divide it into two matching, mirror-image shapes, wherever you draw a line.

See how many symmetrical things you can spot when you look around.

Many living things are symmetrical. Our faces have a symmetrical layout. Animals tend to have the same number of legs, wings, or other parts on each side.

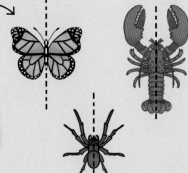

Human-made objects are often symmetrical, too, from buildings and bridges to everyday objects like clothes and bottles.

16

Activity: Missing Sides

Can you fill in the missing half of your face to make a piece of art? What other symmetrical objects could you do this with? Try simple shapes and harder ones, too.

1. Take a photo of yourself looking straight at the camera.

2. Print it on paper. Cut it in half up the middle.

3. Stick it onto another piece of paper. Try to fill in the missing half.

4. If you find it hard to draw it on blank paper, use a ruler to draw a grid.

Around and Around

Is this propeller symmetrical? There's no way it can be divided into two equal sides with a line. However, it has another kind of symmetry called rotational symmetry.

When you rotate or spin the shape part of the way around, it will look the same. For the propeller, you could turn it into four different positions that would all look alike. It has "order 4" symmetry.

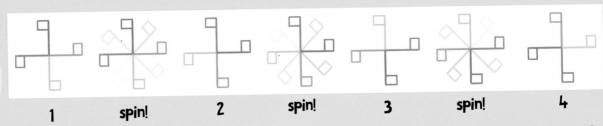

1   spin!   2   spin!   3   spin!   4

Lots of objects around us have rotational symmetry ...

wind spinner or pinwheel

cog

Some objects are symmetrical in both ways. A snowflake, for example, has rotational symmetry and normal symmetry.

18

Activity: Rotational Shapes

You've probably made snowflakes by folding up and cutting paper. You can use the same method for all kinds of other shapes with rotational symmetry, too.

You will need:

- Paper
- Pencil
- Scissors
- A compass, or plates or bowls to draw around

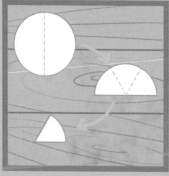

Order 6

1. Snowflakes have order 6 rotational symmetry. To make one, cut out a circle of paper, fold it in half, then fold into thirds, like this.

2. Cut small shapes out of the folded paper, making sure you leave some paper on both sides.

3. Unfold it to see your shape with order 6 rotational symmetry.

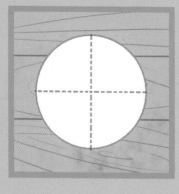

Order 4

To make an order 4 shape, fold a square or circle in half, then fold in half again.

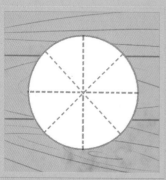

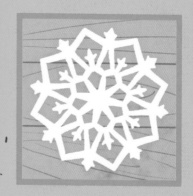

Order 8

To make an order 8 shape, fold a square or circle in half, in half again, and then a third time.

Why Aren't Wheels Square?

Who would want a bike with square or triangular wheels? No one, that's who. It would be impossible to ride. But why? What is it about a circle that makes it the best shape for a wheel?

A circle's diameter is the distance across the middle. Whichever angle you use to measure it, you'll always get the same answer.

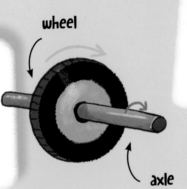

wheel

axle

Vehicles with wheels, such as bikes, cars, and skateboards, have axles to hold the wheel on. The axles are attached to the wheels through the middle.

Now try it with square wheels!

As a wheel rolls along, its middle is always the same distance from the ground ... and you get a smooth ride!

A square is not always the same distance across the middle. It's shorter if you measure it side to side and longer if you measure it corner to corner.

Activity: Trick triangle

Is there any other shape that's always the same width across, like a circle? What do you think?

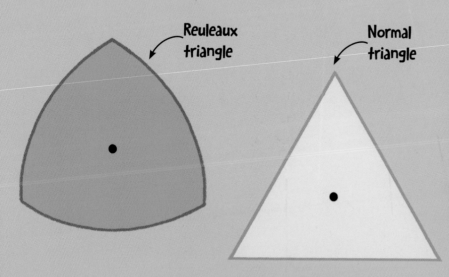

Reuleaux triangle

Normal triangle

With a ruler, try measuring the distance across the normal triangle, through the dot in the middle. As with a square, the distance is different depending on where you measure it.

Then try it with the Reuleaux triangle. What happens?

Reuleaux wheel

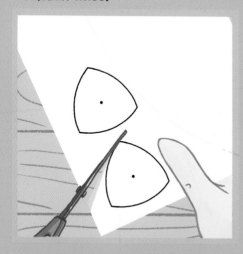

To make Reuleaux triangle wheels, trace this Reuleaux triangle twice onto thick cardstock, and cut out both.

Push a pencil through the middles, and try rolling the wheels along a table.

Do you think it will be a bumpy ride or a smooth ride?

Fitting together

If you wanted to tile a bathroom wall, you'd need tiles that tessellate. That means they have a shape that can fit together with no gaps to cover a space.

Lots of simple shapes tessellate—for example, squares, triangles, and rectangles.

Circles don't, because however you try to fit them together, there will always be gaps.

Honeybees use hexagon shapes to make their honeycomb.

Hexagons tessellate.

Sometimes, two different shapes can tessellate together in a pattern.

It's not just simple shapes that can tessellate. Some strange, curved, and complex shapes can, too.

Activity: Tessellation Test

Here's a selection of shapes, from simple to weird and wonderful.
Can you predict which of them will tessellate, and which won't?

To test them, you can trace the shapes, make
several of each shape out of card or paper,
then try fitting them together.

1

2

3

6

4

5

Check page 60
for
the answers!

The Missing Square

As you probably know, you can figure out the area of a square, rectangle, or triangle if you know how long its sides are. Drawing them on squared graph paper makes this even easier.

For a square or a rectangle, the area of the shape is the length multiplied by the width.

Length 4 squares
Width 4 squares
4 x 4 = 16
Area = 16 squares

Length 18 squares
Width 12 squares
12 x 18 = 216
Area = 216 squares

So the magical puzzle on p. 25 should be easy, right? See if you can solve the mystery!

For a right-angled triangle, it's the base multiplied by the height, divided by two:

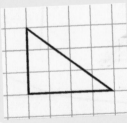

Base 4 squares
Height 3 squares
4 x 3 = 12
12 ÷ 2 = 6
Area = 6 squares

Activity: Where's the Square?

This triangle is made up of a set of simple shapes on a piece of squared paper. You can see how they fit together like a jigsaw.

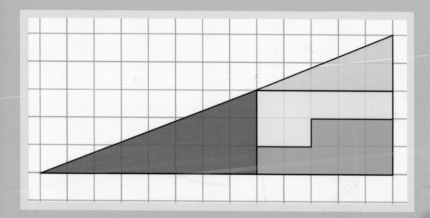

Since it's a right-angled triangle, 13 squares along the base and 5 squares high, we can figure out its area:

13 x 5 = 65
65 ÷ 2 = 32.5 squares

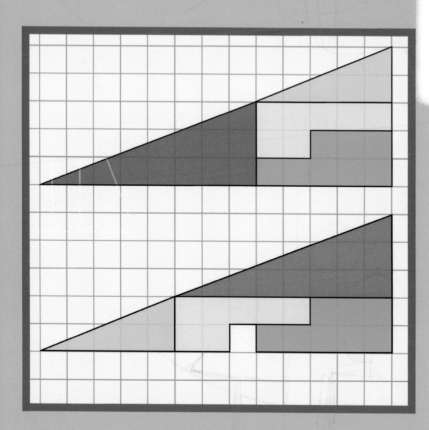

However, if you rearrange the pieces, they don't seem to take up the same space. There's a square that isn't filled in! The area of the triangle has shrunk, and it is now one square smaller. Or IS it?

Can you figure out what happened? If you like, carefully trace the triangle onto paper, and cut it into separate pieces. Then try rearranging them as in the picture.

The explanation is on page 60.

Prime Numbers

Prime numbers are a very mysterious kind of mathematical magic. What is a prime number? It's a whole number that can't be divided by any other numbers except itself and 1.

7 is a prime number
1 x 7 = 7
7 x 1 = 7

6 is not a prime number. You can divide 6 by 2 to get 3, or by 3 to get 2. You can make 6 by multiplying 3 and 2 together. Non-prime numbers above 2, such as 6, are called composite numbers.

6 is a composite number
1 x 6 = 6
6 x 1 = 6

But also ...
2 x 3 = 6
3 x 2 = 6

Can you see a pattern? Can you predict what the next prime number after 100 will be?

1	2	3	4	5	6	7	8	9	10
11	12	13	14	15	16	17	18	19	20
21	22	23	24	25	26	27	28	29	30
31	32	33	34	35	36	37	38	39	40
41	42	43	44	45	46	47	48	49	50
51	52	53	54	55	56	57	58	59	60
61	62	63	64	65	66	67	68	69	70
71	72	73	74	75	76	77	78	79	80
81	82	83	84	85	86	87	88	89	90
91	92	93	94	95	96	97	98	99	100

If you can see a pattern, you really are a math magician! The weird thing about prime numbers is that no one has ever found a reliable pattern or a way of predicting them.

Activity: Prime Snap!

Try playing this prime number card game.

You will need:

- Four sheets of thin cardstock, each about 8.5 x 11 in. (22 x 28 cm)
- Ruler and pencil
- Scissors
- Pen

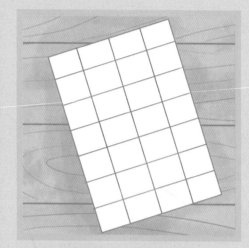

1. Use the ruler and pencil to measure and draw lines dividing each piece of card into 28 rectangles, like this.

2. Cut along the lines to make small playing cards. Write the numbers 1 to 100 on the cards with a pen. (You'll have a few left over.)

3. Shuffle the cards, and hand them out face down between two or more players. Players take turns turning over a card and placing it in the middle of the play area. If the card is a prime number, the first person to yell "Prime!" gets all the cards in the pile. The winner is the first to get all 100 cards.

Graph Graphics

Graphs are a way of showing information in the form of a picture, making it easier to understand and compare facts at a glance.

For example, here's a type of graph called a bar chart. It shows the types of pets a group of people have.

You can see right away that cats and dogs are the most popular pets, and rats are the least popular.

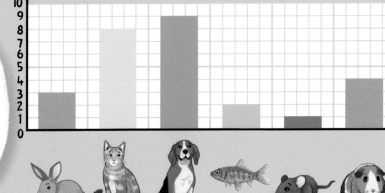

This line graph shows how a person's height has changed during her life.

The units on a graph are written along the bottom of the graph (the X-axis) and up the side (the Y-axis). For example, if x = C and y = 5, the cross shows where x and y numbers meet.

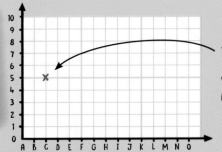

You can mark, or "plot," any point on a graph using the X and Y axis.

Activity: Graph Dot-to-Dot

Test your plotting skills! Plot these x-y coordinates on the graph, numbering them all as in the list. Then connect the dots in order. It will make a picture!

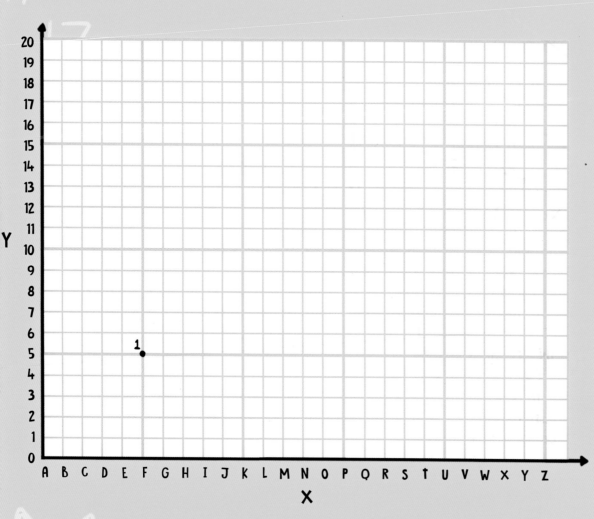

Check page 60 to see if you got it right!

Coordinates: (X, Y)

1.	F5	37.	U6
2.	F6	38.	V6
3.	G6	39.	U5
4.	G7	40.	T5
5.	H10	41.	T6
6.	H11	42.	S7
7.	J13	43.	T9
8.	J15	44.	S7
9.	J13	45.	Q5
10.	H11	46.	O5
11.	G10	47.	P6
12.	G12	48.	Q6
13.	H14	49.	R7
14.	H15	50.	P8
15.	G14	51.	P10
16.	E14	52.	S12
17.	C15	53.	P10
18.	D15	54.	P9
19.	C16	55.	M9
20.	C15	56.	K8
21.	C16	57.	K9
22.	F16	58.	J10
23.	G17	59.	K9
24.	I17	60.	K8
25.	L14	61.	K7
26.	S14	62.	M7
27.	W10	63.	M6
28.	Y12	64.	K6
29.	Z14	65.	J8
30.	Z12	66.	I10
31.	W8	67.	J8
32.	U9	68.	G5
33.	U10	69.	F5
34.	U8		
35.	T7		
36.	U7		

Pieces of the Pie

A pie chart is a type of graph that shows at a glance how something is divided up. Why is it called a pie chart? It's nothing to do with the number Pi (see page 46). It's just because it looks like a pie—round and divided into "slices!"

A pie chart is a circle divided into sections or slices of different sizes to stand for different things. To measure the size of a slice, we use degrees, or °. There are 360° in a whole circle. Half a circle is 180°, a quarter circle is 90°, and so on.

You can measure degrees with a protractor.

Suppose you wanted to make a pie chart showing the different hair types of the 24 people in your class. First, you count the numbers and write them down:

Brown hair: 12 people = half of 24, so this is half the circle, or 180°

Black hair: 6 people = 1/4 of 24, so this is 1/4 of the circle, or 90°

Blond hair: 4 people = 1/6 of 24, so 1/6 of the circle, or 60°

Red hair: 2 people = 1/12 of 24, so 1/12 of the circle, or 30°

Activity: Personality Pie Chart

Create your own personal pie chart showing your likes and interests. What takes up the most space in your brain?

First draw a large circle, and put a dot in the middle.

Make a list of the things you like and spend your time doing or thinking about. Are you into sports, bands, playing an instrument, dancing, reading, being alone, friends, or all of these things?

Choose which things you want to include, and divide up your pie chart, so that the things you like most or do most get the most space.

Fill it in, making it as bright as you like. You can add pictures, too!

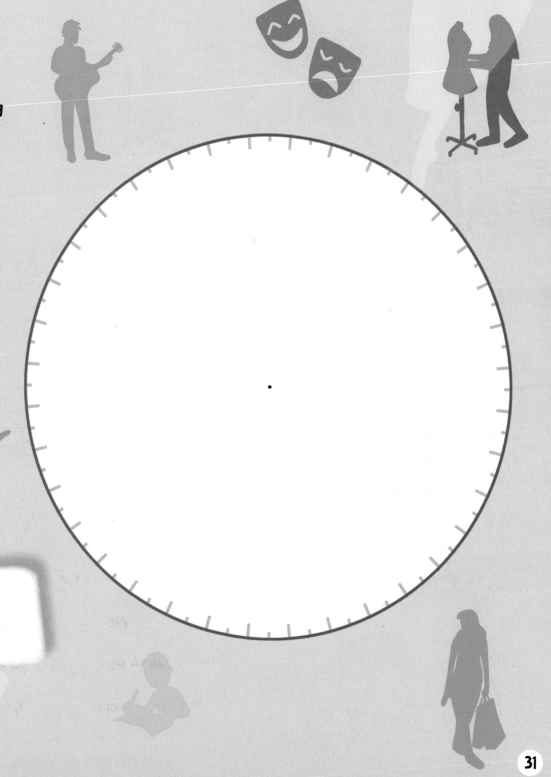

String Shapes

You probably know you can use a compass to draw a circle. A compass works because the distance between the point and the pencil tip stays the same as you draw.

The radius of a circle (the distance between the middle and the edge) is the same all the way around.

Using a compass makes a perfect circle.

But what if you want to draw a really big circle?

Use string! You'll also need a pencil and a thumbtack or drawing pin. Tie one end of the piece of string around the pencil and the other around the pin. Use the pin to hold the string in the middle of the paper and move the pencil around it, holding the string tight. You can draw any size of circle, as long as your string is long enough. You could even draw a huge circle across a sandy beach (using sticks).

Activity: Oval Compass

Did you know you can also use this method to draw ovals?

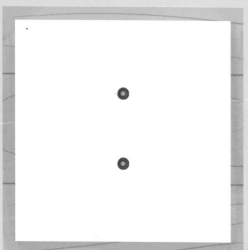

1. Put the paper on the board and stick the two pins or tacks through the paper into the board, about 8 inches (20 cm) apart.

What happens if you use more than two pins or tacks?

2. Cut a piece of string about 16 inches (41 cm) long and tie the ends together to make a loop. Loop the string around the two pins or tacks.

3. Put the tip of the pencil inside the loop and pull it away from the pins or tacks. Draw around the pins with the pencil, keeping the string tight.

Stick or Switch?

This puzzle will leave all your friends confused ... until they know the secret! It's called the Monty Hall problem, because it was used on a game show presented by a man named Monty Hall. Here's how it works.

Monty gives the contestant a choice of three doors. One of the doors hides a valuable prize.

All of the doors have an equal chance of winning. Let's say the contestant picks door 1.

The door the contestant picks remains shut, but Monty Hall opens another door ... which does not have the prize behind it.

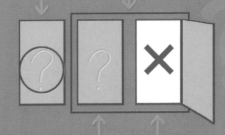

Should the contestant switch and pick door 2 instead? Most people decide to stick with their original choice—it seems as if the chances of winning haven't changed.

WRONG!!! In fact, the contestant has a much better chance of winning by switching.

Choosing one door out of 3 means you have a 1 in 3 chance of winning. After Monty Hall opens a door, there are only two doors left. Switching means you have a 1 in 2 chance of winning.

The door Monty Hall opens is not random. It is never the prize-winning door, and it is never the door the contestant has picked. This means switching your choice of doors really does improve your chances of winning.

Activity: Be Monty Hall

Confused? You're not alone—even mathematicians get confused by this! This puzzle shows how chance and probability can be hard to understand. To see if it's really true, make your own version.

You will need:

- three paper cups
- two small pebbles
- One coin
- Paper and pencil

1. Put the three objects under the cups, remembering where they are.

2. Ask a friend to choose a cup to try to find the coin (but don't pick it up).

3. Lift up another cup that you know has a pebble under it. Ask your friend if she now wants to stick or switch.

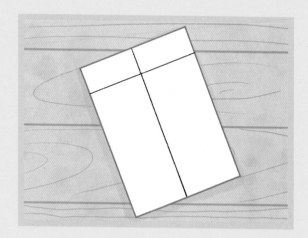

4. Each time, write down what she chose to do, and if she got the coin. Do the test lots of times, and you'll find that switching wins more often!

Sketching Stars

Drawing a star by hand can quickly go wrong. But it's easy to do if you have the magic formula!

To start with, try this simple five-pointed star.

Draw five dots in a circle.

Start at any dot. Skip the next dot and draw a line to the dot after it.

Do the same again—skip the next dot, and draw a line to the dot after it.

And again ...

And again ...

And again ...

You can draw many different stars like this, using one continuous line. All you need to do is:
- Draw a circle of dots—any number of dots.
- Choose a smaller number as the number of dots to count around the side.

There are just two rules:
1. The smaller number must be less than half the number of dots.
2. It must be a number that the first number can't be divided by.

So for 12 dots, you can't have 1, 2, 3, or 4, but you can have 5.

Now start at one dot, count to the fifth dot around the edge, draw a line to that dot, and keep going until you're back to where you started, and you have a star!

Stars like this are called "star polygons." Each type has a name made up of its two numbers—so this is a "12/5" star polygon.

Activity: Star Circles

Here are some circles of dots for you to turn into stars. Follow the formula, and fill in the lines! Then try drawing your own on paper. What's the biggest star polygon you can create?

Polygons and Polyhedrons

When it comes to shapes, math magicians like to use the names "polygons" and "polyhedrons." They're not as confusing as they sound!

Polyhedron means "many faces" (that is, flat sides).

Polygons are flat shapes with straight edges. Lots of familiar shapes are polygons.

Polyhedrons are the 3-D version of polygons. A Polyhedron is a 3-D solid shape, with polygons as its "faces" or sides.

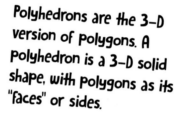

Since polyhedrons are made up of polygons, you can make a polyhedron by folding a flat shape made of polygons. For example, each of these polyhedrons is made from the flat plan beneath it.

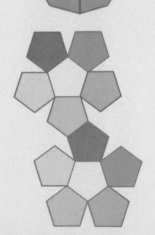

Activity: Polyhedron Patterns

To make your own polyhedrons, copy or trace the templates on this page onto cardstock. Then cut them out, fold them along the black lines, and glue the edges together to make the shapes.

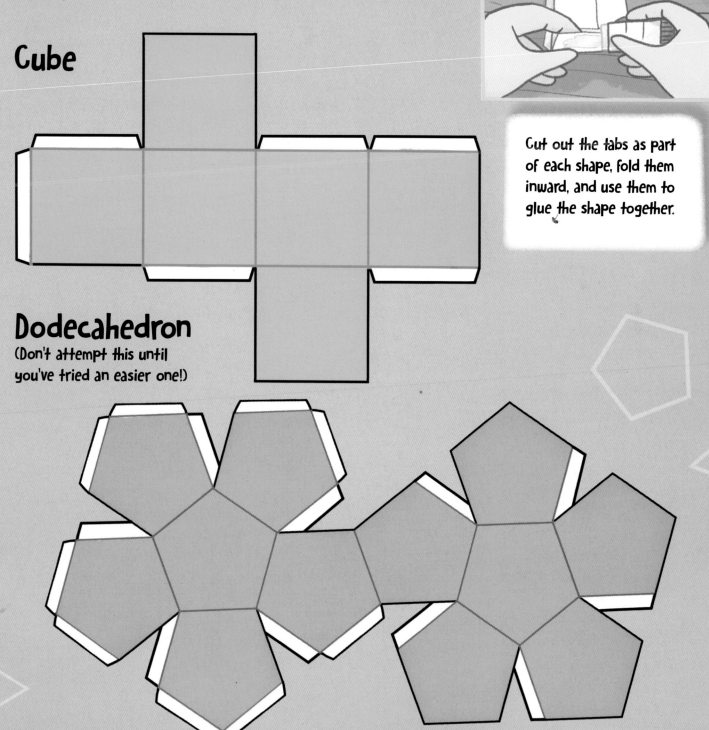

Cube

Cut out the tabs as part of each shape, fold them inward, and use them to glue the shape together.

Dodecahedron
(Don't attempt this until you've tried an easier one!)

Fantastic Fractals

Fractals are a type of mathematical pattern. In a fractal pattern, the same shapes are repeated as smaller and smaller sizes.

Some natural objects grow in fractal patterns. Look at this fern leaf. Its shape is repeated in each of the smaller sections—and the even tinier sections branching off them.

This is a map of streams flowing into larger streams, which then flow into rivers, which flow into larger rivers. It also forms a natural fractal pattern.

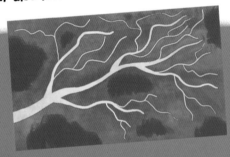

Mathematicians and artists are always coming up with fractal designs and patterns, too. This one is called the Sierpinksi triangle.

You start with a triangle.

You add smaller triangles in all these triangles. Now there are nine triangles ...

You add another, smaller triangle on the middle third of each side.

And so on ... and so on

Activity: Fractal Trees

Many trees grow in a pattern resembling a fractal. The trunk divides into main branches, which divide into smaller branches, which divide into smaller branches, and so on, until there are hundreds of tiny twigs.

Try drawing a tree fractal on paper using the steps on the right.

Then try drawing a whole tree in this space, using the fractal method. What happens if you draw three or four branches each time, instead of two?

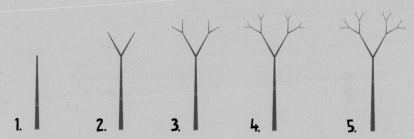

1.   2.   3.   4.   5.

Bigger and Bigger

An Indian legend tells the story of the man who invented chess. The king loved the new game and summoned the inventor to see him.

"I want to repay you for this wonderful invention," said the king. "You can have any reward you like."

The man thought about it and then said:

"All I ask is one grain of rice for the first square on the chess board, two for the second, four for the third, and so on. Double the number of grains each time, until you've used up every square on the board."

The king agreed, and began measuring out the rice. How many grains do you think he needed?

Wait a minute ... ! At first, this request seems reasonable. But, as the king found, doubling a number over and over again means it soon gets very, VERY big.

The numbers are small at first, but they soon become huge!

A chessboard has 64 squares. For the 64th square, the king would need

9,223,372,036,854,775,808

grains of rice. That's over 9 million billion (a LOT more rice than the king had).

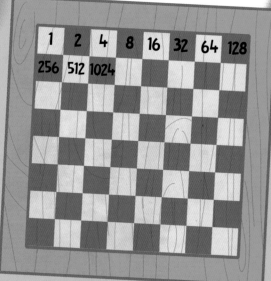

| 1 | 2 | 4 | 8 | 16 | 32 | 64 | 128 |
| 256 | 512 | 1024 | | | | | |

Activity: the Paper Folding Challenge

The king failed the chessboard challenge, but can you manage the folding paper challenge? It's another way of creating exponential growth. All you need is a sheet of thin paper. Newspaper is perfect.

Your challenge is to fold the paper in half, then in half again, and again ... eight times in total.

Can you do it? Try challenging a friend to try it, too!

Each time you fold the paper, its thickness is doubled. It quickly becomes very hard to keep folding.

Curves from Straight Lines

Can you make a curve using only straight lines? There is a way, using a special mathematical method. It also makes amazing patterns.

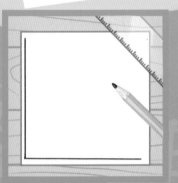

Draw two lines at right angles, like this.

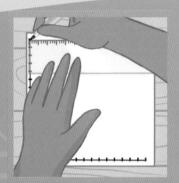

Use the ruler to mark evenly spaced dots along both lines. Make the same number of dots along each line—there are 15 in this example.

Now you draw a line from the first dot on one line, to the last dot on the other line.

Then move along one dot on each line, and draw another line between them.

It's not perfect, since it's made of short straight sections, but it looks curved.

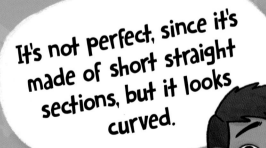

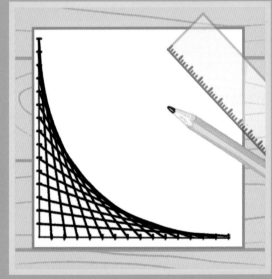

Keep going in the same way, and the curve appears! This is a parabolic curve.

Activity: String Curves

Instead of drawing lines, you can use string to make a curve. Using different angles and shapes, you can make all kinds of parabolic curves and patterns.

⚠ Pushing needles through things can be dangerous—take care not to hurt yourself! Ask an adult to make sure you're doing this safely.

You will need:

- Stiff cardstock
- Ruler and pencil
- Thin string or embroidery thread
- Scissors
- A large needle

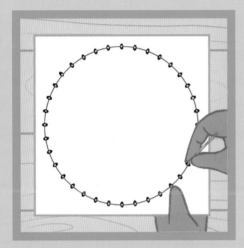

1. Draw lines or shapes on your cardstock and mark with evenly spaced dots. Push the needle through each dot to make a hole.

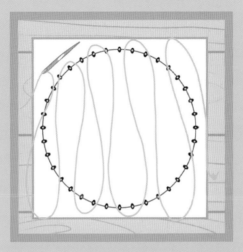

2. Cut about 20 inches (51 cm) of string or thread and thread it in your needle (ask an adult to help if you need to). Tie a knot in the end.

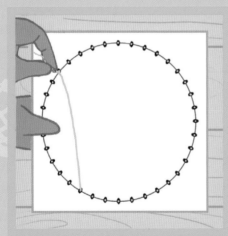

3. Push your needle through from the back of the cardstock into the first hole, then sew through another hole to make a line.

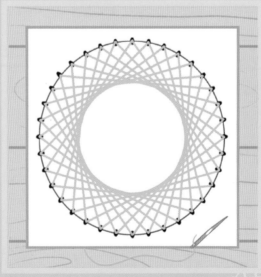

4. Keep sewing in and out of the cardstock to make the lines, like this.

Peculiar Pi

Pi is a number, but it's not a number that you can write down or say out loud. Unlike 2, or 106, or 7.5, pi is a number without an end. If you started telling someone pi, you'd never stop. You'd be describing it forever!

What is pi? Pi comes from something quite normal and familiar—the circle. It's what you get if you divide the circumference of a circle (the distance around the edge) by the diameter (the distance across the middle).

3 diameters

diameter

1 diameter

2 diameters

The circumference divided by the diameter equals:

3.14159265358979323846264338327950288419716939937510582097494459230781640628620899862803482534211707679 ...

This number is pi—or at least, the first part of it. Pi is a decimal number that goes on forever. To make it easier to use, we usually round it down to 3.14.

It doesn't matter how big or small a circle is—divide the circumference by the diameter, and you'll always get pi.

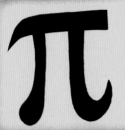

π There's also an even easier way to write down pi, using this symbol.

Activity: Practical Pi

Pi is very useful—it can often help us figure out how to do everyday things. Try these real-life pi puzzles.

! We've given the measurements in both imperial (inches) and metric (cm), but make sure you use the same measurements throughout! the answers are on page 61.

Chocolate box diameter 4 inches (10 cm)

Round gifts

Ali is giving his sister a round box of chocolates for her birthday.

How long a piece of wrapping paper does Ali need to reach around the box?

Holly's head diameter 6 inches (15 cm)

Paper crown

Holly is playing the queen in the school play, so she's making a paper crown.

How long should the strip of paper be to reach around her head?

Grandpa's cake

Grandpa is making a cake with chocolate balls around the edge.

the balls are 1/2 inch (1 cm) across. How many does he need?

Cake diameter 12 inches (30 cm)

Eureka!

Archimedes was an ancient Greek scientist, inventor, and general genius. He's famous for leaping out of the bathtub shouting "Eureka!" ("I've got it!"). Why? According to the legend, the bath water had helped him crack a tricky problem.

The story goes that the king had paid a craftsman to make a golden crown. But he was worried that instead of using solid gold, the craftsman had sneakily mixed in some much cheaper silver. So he asked Archimedes to find out.

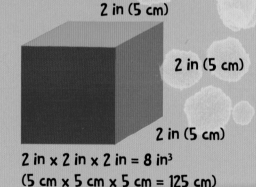

Archimedes knew that gold is much denser than silver—it weighs more. That meant that a solid gold crown of a particular weight would have less volume and take up less space than a crown with silver mixed in.

Archimedes could weigh the crown, but he also needed to know the volume.

It's easy to figure out the volume of a simple shape like a cube, but the crown was a random, complicated shape.

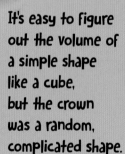

2 in (5 cm)

2 in (5 cm)

2 in (5 cm)

2 in x 2 in x 2 in = 8 in³
(5 cm x 5 cm x 5 cm = 125 cm)

As Archimedes climbed into his bath, he saw the water rise. He suddenly realized that his body had pushed the water up. He could measure the crown's volume in the same way—by putting it in water and seeing how much the water level rose. Archimedes tested equal weights of gold and silver, along with the crown, and realized that the crown was not pure gold, but a mixture of gold and silver.

Activity: The Archimedes Method

The Archimedes story is a very old one, and no one knows if it's really true. But it definitely IS true that you can easily measure volume in this way. Try it!

You will need:
- A large measuring jug or container
- Water
- Odd-shaped, waterproof objects to measure, such as spoons or plastic animals
- Pen, paper, and calculator

Which of these 5 objects do you think has the largest volume? The answers are on page 61.

1. Fill the measuring container with water to around halfway. Write down the level of the water.

2. Put your object into the water, making sure it's completely submerged. Write down the level the water rises to.

3. Subtract the level you started with from the new level to find the volume of the object.

Digital Image

Computers do all their calculations using patterns of 0s and 1s. This is called "binary code." They also store other information that way. We often call it "digital" information, meaning it's in the form of numbers.

When you type letters and symbols into a computer, the computer converts them into binary code.

1010011101
01101010110
0101010010

Whether you're playing a song or recording a voice memo, the sounds are stored in the computer as patterns of 0s and 1s.

The key presses you use to play games are converted into digital signals to make the game work.

All the pictures you see on screens are stored in patterns of binary code—even detailed photos, complex pictures, and videos.

Activity: Decode the Image

To turn a series of binary numbers back into a picture, the computer has to decode them. It reads the binary code and sends signals to the screen to display different colors in the different pixels (the tiny dots that make up the screen).

Try decoding this binary code to make a picture.
Each pair of digits (0s and 1s) stands for a different color:

00 = white   11 = black
01 = yellow   100 = red
10 = blue

Start at the beginning of the code. Take the first two digits, check what they stand for, and fill in the first square in the top row of grid that color. Then put the color for the next two digits in the next square, and so on. When you get to the end of a row in the grid, just start the next row.

```
00  00  01  01  01   01   01  01  00  00
00  01  01  01  01   01   01  01  01  00
01  01  10  10  01   01   10  10  01  01
01  01  10  10  01   01   10  10  01  01
01  01  01  01  01   01   01  01  01  01
01  11  01  01  01   01   01  01  11  01
01  01  11  01  01   01   01  11  01  01
01  01  01  11  100 100  11  01  01  01
00  01  01  01  100 100  01  01  01  00
00  00  01  01  01   01   01  01  00  00
```

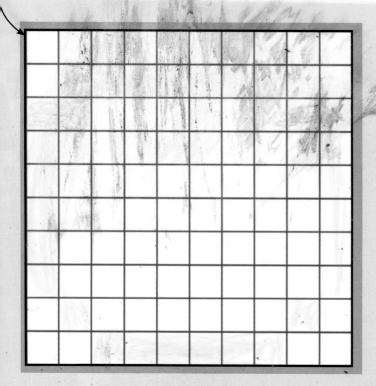

To make it easier, mark off each pair of digits with a line so you don't lose your place.

Now try writing the code for this penguin!
It's fairly long, but stick with it ... the answers for both code puzzles are on page 61.

51

Body Numbers

Do you ever wonder why the "foot" is a unit of measurement? Is it anything to do with actual feet? The answer is yes! When people first started measuring things in prehistoric times, there was no fixed measuring system. So they used their own body parts.

Of course, there's a problem with this. These measurements are not the same for everyone, so it's hard to be accurate.

Several of these body part units became widely used.

A **hand** was the width across a man's hand—it's still used to measure horses.

A **thumb** was the thickness of a man's thumb. It later became known as the inch.

A **cubit** or ell was the distance from the elbow to the fingertips.

A **fathom** was the distance between a man's fingertips if he stretched his arms wide.

A **foot** was the average length of a man's foot.

So, over time, people standardized them. A foot is now a standard measure—12 inches, or just over 30 cm. That's the length of a typical ruler.

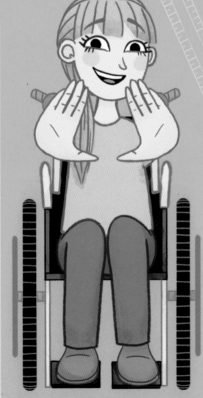

Activity: Your Body Numbers

Using a tape measure, try measuring your own foot, fathom, hand, cubit, and thumb. Are they the same as other people's? What about measuring some other children or a family member?

My foot ————————————

My fathom ————————————

My hand ————————————

My cubit ————————————

My thumb ————————————

Although humans vary a lot, each person's measurements often follow a strangely similar pattern.

Height = distance from fingertip to fingertip when arms are outstretched

Thickness of one wrist = distance from middle fingertip to thumb tip

Length of foot = distance from tip of elbow to wrist

Width of one eye = distance between eyes

Number Brain

Did you know that your brain is always doing math—whether you're thinking about it or not? To make sense of the world and keep you safe, your brain has to do constant calculations.

Humans have two eyes that see things from two slightly different angles. The brain uses the difference between them to calculate how far away things are and see in 3-D.

If you see a small group of objects, you count them at a glance, without thinking. Try looking at these pictures for just a second and saying how many apples there are. How many limes? How many peaches?

You probably don't need to actually count the limes or the apples. Your brain just does it for you!

If you start to tip over, you stick an arm or leg out, just enough to balance you again. You don't think about it, but your brain calculates the right direction and distance.

Activity: Which Direction?

Test yourself, or someone with good hearing, with this math challenge. Don't worry, your brain does all the work!

You will need:

- A chair
- A large space
- A friend or family member to help

1. Sit on the chair, facing away from the helper.

2. Ask the other person to take their shoes off to make them extra-quiet. Now ask them to stand behind you, about 10 feet (3 m) away.

3. They should then move silently to the left or right, then clap once. You have to point to where the clap came from.

Easy, isn't it? But to do this, your brain has to do a difficult calculation.

The sound takes slightly different amounts of time to reach each ear.

Your brain measures this difference and calculates the angle.

You "sense" where the sound is coming from—thanks to math!

Monster Numbers

What's the biggest number that can possibly exist? In math, you can write down this idea of never-endingness, or "infinity." It looks like this: "∞." As you can see, it's like a figure 8 on its side, and it makes an endless loop that goes around and around forever.

The sequence of numbers is infinite, which means they go on forever. Whatever the biggest number you can possibly imagine is, you could always add 1 to it. And another 1, and another—forever!

However, mathematicians have come up with some seriously huge numbers. The most famous is the googol. (Not the Google—the googol. The googol was invented first, and the search engine Google was named after it!) A googol is 1 with 100 zeroes after it. It looks like this:

$$10,000,000,000,000,000,000,000,000,000,000,$$
$$000,000,000,000,000,000,000,000,000,000,000,$$
$$000,000,000,000,000,000,000,000,000,000,000$$

It was a 9-year-old boy, Milton Sirotta, who came up with the name "Googol." His uncle, mathematician Edward Kasner, asked what he should call a 1 with 100 zeros after it, and that was Milton's answer.

Activity: Big Numbers Quiz

Try these real-life big number questions ... Take a guess,
then turn to page 61 to see how close you were.

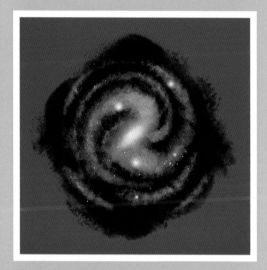

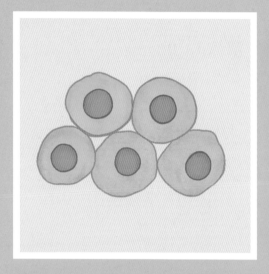

1. How many stars are there in our Galaxy, the Milky Way?

A. About 250 billion.
B. About 10 billion.
C. About a billion billion.

2. How many cells are there in the average human body?

A. About 150 trillion.
B. About 37 trillion.
C. About 4 trillion.

3. How many grains of sand are there in the world?

A. About 7 quintillion.
B. About 4 octillion.
C. About 1.5 googol.

These numbers are big
... but none of them is
as big as a googol!

10,000,000,000,000,000,
000,000,000,000,000,000,
000,000,000,000,000,000,
000,000,000,000,000,000,
000,000,000,000,000,000,
000,000,000,000

Pop Quiz

Have you been paying attention? Test your math knowledge here! Write down your answers on the following page.

1. True or false? In a magic square, the rows and columns and diagonals all add up to consecutive numbers.

2. True or false? A Möbius strip has one edge and one surface.

3. If the shorter sides of a golden rectangle are 4 inches (10cm) long, how long will the longer sides be?

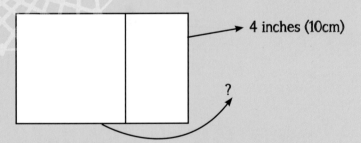

→ 4 inches (10cm)

?

4. Use the cipher on page 14 to work out this message:

9   12 15 22 5   19 5 3 18 5 20   3 15 4 5 19

5. Do these snowflakes have order 5 or order 6 symmetry?

6. Which of these are prime numbers:

4, 5, 14, 15, 30, 51, 79, 89, 100.

7. All the children on Holly's soccer team picked a piece of fruit for an after-game snack. Which is the most popular? How many children chose to eat an apple?

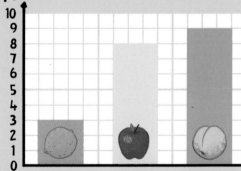

8. Ali bought a pack of stickers with his allowance. This pie chart shows how many there were of each kind. If there are 24 stickers in the pack in total, how many are heart-shaped stickers?

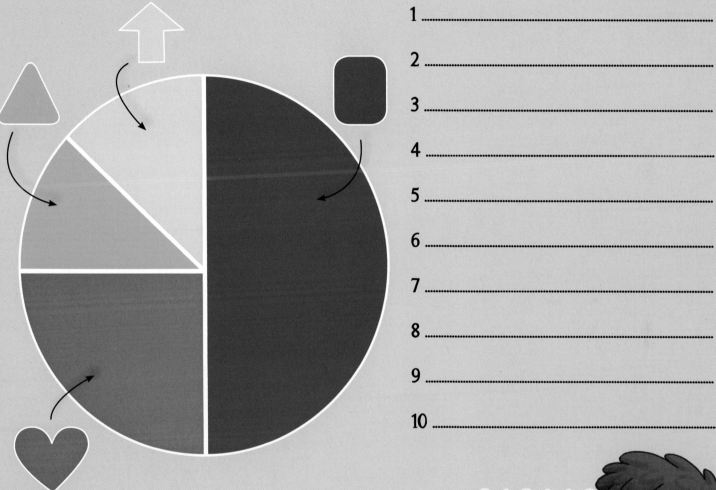

9. True or false? It's possible to fold a piece of regular newspaper in half 34 times.

10. True or false? A "foot" is the same length as an average child's foot.

Write down your answers here, and check them on page 61.

1 ....

2 ....

3 ....

4 ....

5 ....

6 ....

7 ....

8 ....

9 ....

10 ....

Answers

P. 23

1, 2, 5, and 6 tessellate perfectly in a continuous pattern. 3 and 4 (shown below) need an extra shape to be able to tessellate. 3 needs a square and 4 needs a triangle.

P. 7

A:

3	2	7
8	4	0
1	6	5

B:

5	11	2
3	6	9
10	1	7

C:

3	14	15	2
8	9	12	5
10	7	6	11
13	4	1	16

P. 11

6 x 7 = 42   9 x 8 = 72
8 x 10 = 80   10 x 6 = 60
7 x 9 = 63   7 x 10 = 70
9 x 10 = 90   9 x 9 = 81
6 x 8 = 48   6 x 9 = 54

P. 25

In fact, this isn't actually a math problem—it's an optical illusion! If you hold a ruler along the longest side of the triangle in the first picture, you'll find it isn't actually completely straight. It bends inward very slightly. You don't notice this because you're distracted by the grid squares and the two separate triangle shapes. When you rearrange the pieces, the red and blue triangles swap places, and this means that the long side of the triangle ends up bulging outward slightly instead. The extra space this takes up is the same as the area of the missing square.

P. 29

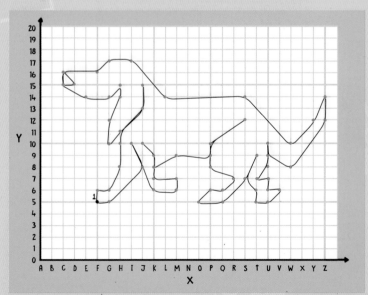

p. 47

Ali will need 12.56 inches or 31.90 cm of wrapping paper.

Holly will need 18.84 inches or 47.85 cm of paper for her crown.

Grandpa will need 94 balls if he's making a 30-cm cake with 1-cm balls. He will need 75 balls if he's making a 12-inch cake with 1/2-inch balls.

p. 49

Of these 5 objects, the coin has the smallest volume, then the spoon, the golf ball, and the dinosaur. The orange has the biggest volume.

p. 51

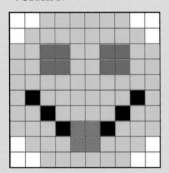

Bonus penguin code from page 51:
00 00 00 00 00 00 00 01 01 01 01 01 01 00 00 00 00 00 00 00 00
00 00 00 00 00 00 01 01 01 01 01 01 01 01 00 00 00 00 00 00 00
00 00 00 00 00 01 00 00 01 01 01 01 00 00 01 00 00 00 00 00 00
00 00 00 00 01 00 00 00 00 01 01 00 00 00 00 00 01 00 00 00 00
00 00 00 00 01 00 01 01 00 01 01 00 01 01 00 01 00 00 00 00 00
00 00 00 00 01 00 01 01 00 01 01 00 01 01 00 01 00 00 00 00 00
00 00 00 00 01 00 00 00 01 01 00 00 00 00 01 00 00 00 00 00
00 00 00 00 01 00 00 00 02 02 02 02 00 00 00 01 00 00 00 00 00
00 00 00 00 01 01 00 00 00 02 02 00 00 00 01 01 00 00 00 00 00
00 00 00 01 01 01 00 00 00 00 00 00 00 00 01 01 01 00 00 00
00 00 01 01 01 00 00 00 00 00 00 00 00 00 00 01 01 01 00 00 00
00 00 01 01 01 00 00 00 00 00 00 00 00 00 00 01 01 01 00 00 00
00 01 01 01 01 00 00 00 00 00 00 00 00 00 00 01 01 01 01 00
00 01 01 01 01 00 00 00 00 00 00 00 00 00 00 01 01 01 01 00
01 01 01 01 01 00 00 00 00 00 00 00 00 00 00 01 01 01 01 01
01 01 01 01 01 00 00 00 00 00 00 00 00 00 00 01 01 01 01 01
00 01 00 01 01 00 00 00 00 00 00 00 00 00 00 01 01 00 01 00
00 00 00 01 01 00 00 00 00 00 00 00 00 00 00 01 01 00 00 00
00 00 00 01 01 00 00 00 00 00 00 00 00 00 00 01 01 00 00 00
00 00 00 01 01 00 00 00 00 00 00 00 00 00 00 01 01 00 00 00
00 00 00 00 01 01 00 00 00 00 00 00 00 00 01 01 00 00 00 00
00 00 00 00 01 01 00 00 00 00 00 00 00 00 01 01 00 00 00 00
00 00 00 00 00 01 01 01 01 01 01 01 01 01 00 00 00 00 00
00 00 00 00 00 03 03 03 00 00 00 00 03 03 03 00 00 00 00 00 00
00 00 00 00 03 03 03 03 03 00 00 03 03 03 03 03 00 00 00 00

PP. 56–57

1. A. There are about 250 billion stars in our galaxy. That's a very rough number though!
2. B. There are about 37 trillion cells in an average body. Every body is different, but they all have roughly this number of cells.
3. A. There are about 7 quintillion grains of sand in the world.

PP. 58–59

1. False. They all add up to the SAME number.
2. True.
3. 6.47 inches (16.43 cm).
4. I LOVE SECRET CODES
5. The snowflakes have order 6 symmetry.
6. The only prime numbers from this selection are: 5, 79, and 89.
7. Peaches are the most popular choice of snack, and 8 children chose to eat an apple.
8. There are 6 heart-shaped stickers.
9. False. You can only fold regular paper in half 8 times before it gets too thick. However, in 2002, schoolgirl Britney Gallivan, of Pomona, California, folded a piece of paper in half 12 times. It was a VERY long piece of paper though—more than 3/4 mile (1 km) long!
10. False. A "foot" is the same length as an average MAN's foot.

Glossary

Angle The space between two intersecting lines, close to the point where they meet (usually measured in degrees).

Axis An imaginary straight line passing through the middle of a symmetrical solid.

Bar chart/bar graph A diagram where numerical values are shown by the height or length of lines or rectangles.

Base (with a number) The numbers that are used in a counting system (e.g., base 2 uses two numbers, 0 and 1).

Base (of a shape) The bottom line of a 2-D shape or the surface a 3-D shape stands on.

Binary A system of counting or notation that has 2 as its base.

Calculator A machine used for making mathematical calculations.

Cipher wheel A tool made of two concentric circles, used for making and breaking encrypted messages.

Circumference The distance around the edge of a circle.

Compass A two-armed instrument used for drawing circles.

Composite number A whole number that can be made by multiplying other whole numbers.

Coordinates A set of values that show a position on a graph.

Cube A symmetrical 3-D shape with six sides made of equal squares.

Decimal number A number with a decimal point followed by digits showing a value smaller than 1.

Decode Convert a coded message into an understandable one.

Degrees A unit of measurement of angles, shown by this symbol: °. There are 360° in a full circle and 90° in a right angle.

Density The weight of an object compared to the amount of space it fills.

Diameter The distance of a straight line from side to side passing through the midpoint of a circle.

Digit Any of the numbers 0 to 9.

Encode Convert a message into coded form.

Exponential growth Growth of a value in proportion to its size (so, the bigger the number the bigger the growth).

Formula A rule written with mathematical symbols.

Fractal A repeated geometric pattern.

Golden ratio The number approximately equal to 1.618, describing a special way of dividing a line into two parts.

Googol 1 followed by 100 zeros.

Hexagon A six-sided flat shape.

Inch A unit of length. There are 12 inches in a foot.

Infinity Something that goes on and on with no bounds or outer edge.

Magic square A square where the numbers in each row, column, and diagonal total the same.

Mental arithmetic Calculations done in the mind, without using a calculator or writing down the numbers.

Möbius strip A surface with one continuous side (made by joining the ends of a rectangle after twisting one end).

Multiple The result of multiplying a number by a whole number.

Multiply To add a number to itself a specified number of times.

Parabolic curve A special arch-shaped curve made from straight lines.

Parchment A writing material made from prepared animal skin (e.g., sheep or goat).

Pi The number reached by dividing the circumference of a circle by its diameter (approximately 3.14). It is a constant, or unchanging, number.

Pie chart/pie graph A circular graph in which each section represents a proportion of the whole.

Pixels Tiny lit-up areas on a screen that combine to make an image.

Polygon A 2-D shape with straight sides.

Polyhedron A 3-D shape made up of flat faces.

Prime number A number that can only be divided by itself or 1.

Probability The branch of mathematics that studies how likely something is to happen.

Protractor An instrument for measuring angles.

Radius A straight line from the middle of a circle to its edge.

Ratio A way of comparing two or more numbers.

Reuleaux triangle A shape made when three circles cross. It looks like a triangle with round sides.

Right angle An angle of 90° (e.g., the corner of a square, or a quarter of a circle).

Right-angled triangle A triangle with one angle of 90°.

Rotational symmetry When a shape stays the same if you turn it.

Scytale A cylindrical tool used for making and breaking codes.

Symmetry A shape stays the same whether you flip, slide, or turn it.

Tessellation A pattern made of shapes that fit exactly with no gaps or overlap.

Three-dimensional Having three dimensions, such as a cube or pyramid. Also known as 3-D

Math is magical!
Prepare to be amazed!

Explore how math is an important part of everyday life with this colorful activity book that shows you interesting and meaningful ways to use numbers.

Have fun with more than 25 awesome math activities with easy-to-follow instructions:

- Master a mind reading trick
- Create secret codes
- Play a prime number game
- Create a personality pie chart
- Draw fractal trees
- Make a 3-dimensional Möbius strip
- and lots more!

Check out these other I can be books!

I can be a
Science Detective
Claudia Martin

I can be a
Rocket Scientist
Anna Claybourne

I can be an
Awesome Inventor
Anna Claybourne

www.doverpublications.com

$9.99 USA   PRINTED IN CHINA
ISBN-13: 978-0-486-83922-6
ISBN-10: 0-486-83922-2
50999
9 780486 839226

JUVENILE NONFICTION/ACTIVITY BOOKS